Let's Go Shopping!

Adriana Rincón
and Esperanza Bejarano
Illustrated by Fabricio Vanden Broeck

 **HAMPTON-BROWN BOOKS**
MANY CULTURES, MANY LANGUAGES...MANY POSSIBILITIES!™

What do they sell
at the bakery?

Bread.

What do they sell
at the fruit stand?

Fruit.

What do they sell
at the tortilla shop?

Tortillas.

What do they sell
at the supermarket?
Everything!